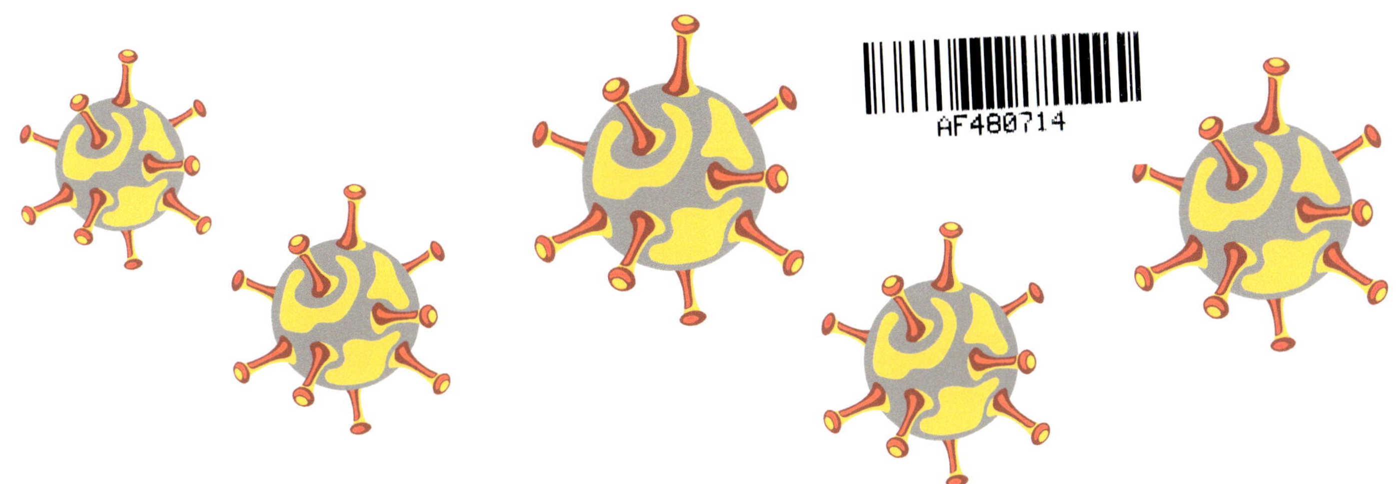

The Historical Events of Covid-19

QUARANTINE

Jessica Wilson

For the brave men and women and boys and girls who endured the many hardships, challenges and loss of loved ones to the coronavirus pandemic. A special dedication to my Aunt Lois who lost her life to COVID-19.

The Historical Events of COVID-19 Quarantine by Jessica L. Wilson
Published by KDP via Wilson Collective, LLC.
www.writermom.org

ISBN: 9798645392932

In the year 2020,

a pandemic hit the nation.

My family spent months at home,

in our first required staycation.

The virus began in China,
country to country and air to sea.

The world as we knew it
was taken by all things Covid-19.

In small towns and big cities,

STAY AT HOME orders were put in place.

PEOPLE WORE GLOVES ON THEIR HANDS
AND MASKS ON THEIR FACE.

"No school," I heard,
and I shouted, "Hurray!"

But then I found out

No friends and no graduation day.

RESTAURANTS AND BUSINESSES
CLOSED THEIR DOORS.

WITH HOPES THAT ALL FAMILIES

WOULD NOT IGNORE.

NO STORES, NO PARKS,

NO POOLS, NOR PUBLIC PLACES.

TAKE-OUT FOOD WAS ALLOWED
BUT ONLY FROM MASKED FACES.

Grocery stores stayed open
But many items couldn't be found.

SOME HAD TO GET CREATIVE WITH NO TOILET PAPER AROUND!

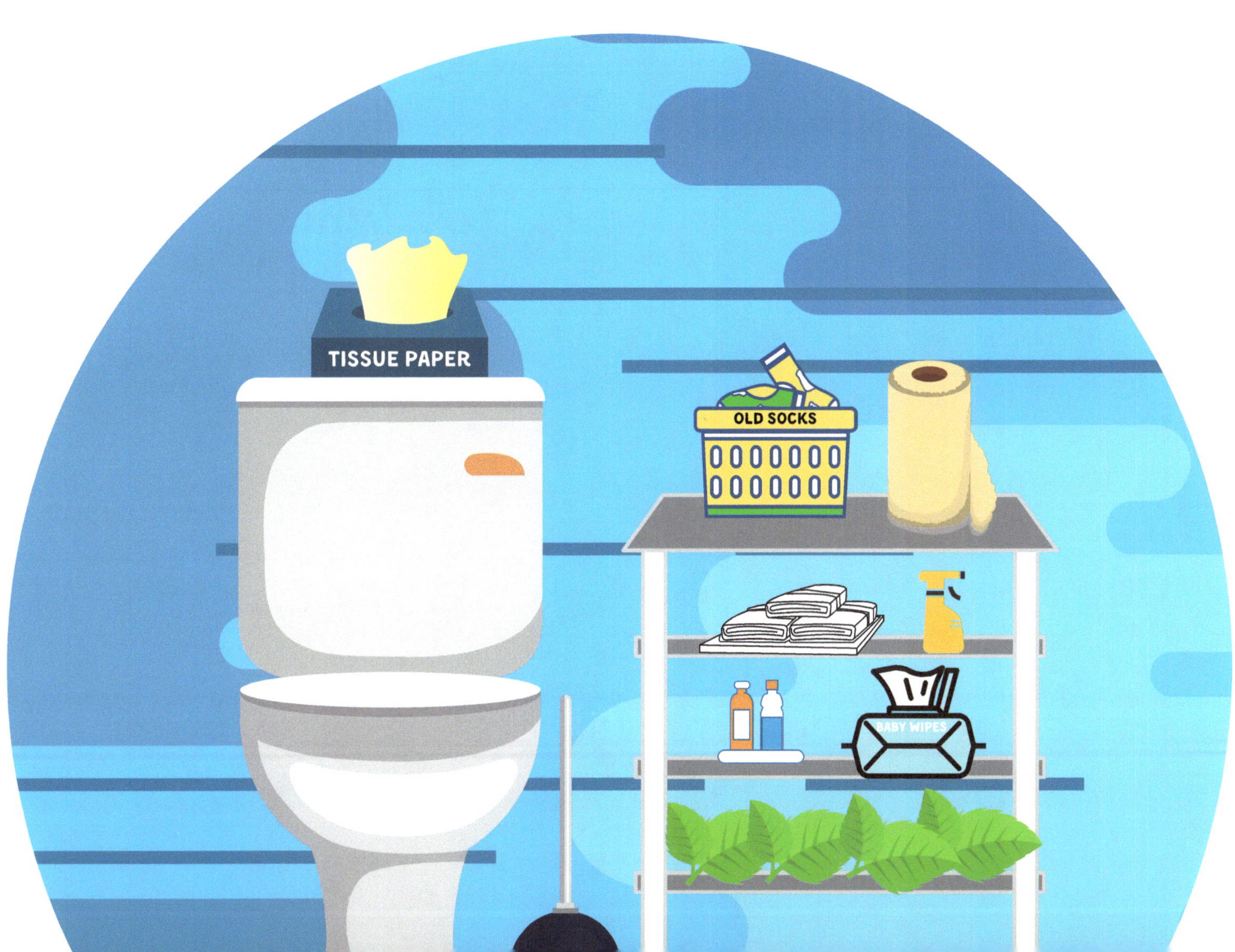

ESSENTIAL WORKERS WERE THE TRUE HEROES;

DOCTORS, NURSES, POLICE TO NAME A FEW.

THEY WORKED HARD TO KEEP US SAFE
UNTIL THE COVID BREAKTHROUGH.

"SOCIAL DISTANCING" WAS REQUIRED,
NO TRAVEL, NO TRIPS, NOR VISITS.

VIDEO CALLS AND ONLINE CHATTING

HELPED LIFT ALL OUR SPIRITS.

THE GOOD CAME OUT IN YOUNG AND OLD;

PACKAGES, BIRTHDAY TRAINS AND LETTERS.

WE REACHED OUT TO

FRIENDS AND FAMILY

AND THAT MADE

THINGS MUCH BETTER.

Daddy and mommy worked from home,
And I did school online.

EVERYTHING WAS

A LITTLE CRAZY,

BUT DAD SAID, "WE'LL

BE JUST FINE."

OTHER VIRUSES HAVE COME BEFORE,
THE WORLD WAS FORCED TO FIGHT.

BUT ALL GOT BACK TO NORMAL

AND EVERYTHING TURNED OUT ALL RIGHT.

THE VIRUS DID PASS,

AND OUR NATION GREW STRONGER.

TOGETHER WE STOOD UNITED,

HAVING NO FEAR ANY LONGER.